P9-DMQ-125

Received

LOWER COLUMBIA REVIEW

T 35014

AL 2,9
Pts ,5

SandCastle™

Animal Tales

Cow Licks

Pam Scheunemann

Illustrated by Anne Haberstroh

Consulting Editor, Diane Craig, M.A./Reading Specialist

ABDO
Publishing Company

CARROLLS ELEMENTARY SCHOOL LIBRARY
3902 OLD PACIFIC HIGHWAY S.
KELSO, WASHINGTON 98626

07-026 Bk. Review 10.00

Published by ABDO Publishing Company, 4940 Viking Drive, Edina, Minnesota 55435.

Copyright © 2006 by Abdo Consulting Group, Inc. International copyrights reserved in all countries. No part of this book may be reproduced in any form without written permission from the publisher. SandCastle™ is a trademark and logo of ABDO Publishing Company.

Printed in the United States.

Credits
Edited by: Pam Price
Curriculum Coordinator: Nancy Tuminelly
Cover and Interior Design and Production: Mighty Media
Photo Credits: BananaStock Ltd., Digital Vision, Photodisc, ShutterStock

Library of Congress Cataloging-in-Publication Data

Scheunemann, Pam, 1955-
    Cow licks / Pam Scheunemann ; illustrated by Anne Haberstroh.
       p. cm. -- (Fact & fiction. Animal tales)
    Summary: Mrs. O'Leary, owner of Cool Licks ice cream shop, teaches young Dottie to make ice cream, too, so that there will be enough for the Moo Town Festival. Includes facts about cows.
    ISBN 1-59679-929-3 (hardcover)
    ISBN 1-59679-930-7 (paperback)
    [1. Ice cream parlors--Fiction. 2. Ice cream, ices, etc.--Fiction. 3. Cows--Fiction.] I. Haberstroh, Anne, ill. II. Title. III. Series.
    PZ7.S34424Cow 2006
    [E]--dc22

                                                                                            2005027827

SandCastle Level: Fluent

SandCastle™ books are created by a professional team of educators, reading specialists, and content developers around five essential components—phonemic awareness, phonics, vocabulary, text comprehension, and fluency—to assist young readers as they develop reading skills and strategies and increase their general knowledge. All books are written, reviewed, and levels for guided reading, early reading intervention, and Accelerated Reader® programs for use in shared, guided, and independent reading and writing activities to support a balanced approach to literacy instruction. The SandCastle™ series has four levels that correspond to early literacy development. The levels help teachers and parents select appropriate books for young readers.

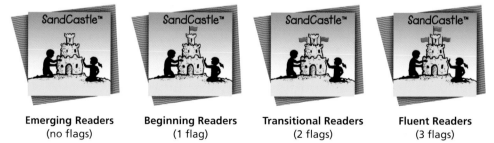

Emerging Readers	Beginning Readers	Transitional Readers	Fluent Readers
(no flags)	(1 flag)	(2 flags)	(3 flags)

These levels are meant only as a guide. All levels are subject to change.

FACT & FiCTiON

This series provides early fluent readers the opportunity to develop reading comprehension strategies and increase fluency. These books are appropriate for guided, shared, and independent reading.

FACT The left-hand pages incorporate realistic photographs to enhance readers' understanding of informational text.

FiCTiON The right-hand pages engage readers with an entertaining, narrative story that is supported by whimsical illustrations.

The Fact and Fiction pages can be read separately to improve comprehension through questioning, predicting, making inferences, and summarizing. They can also be read side-by-side, in spreads, which encourages students to explore and examine different writing styles.

FACT OR FiCTiON? This fun quiz helps reinforce students' understanding of what is real and not real.

SPEED READ The text-only version of each section includes word-count rulers for fluency practice and assessment.

GLOSSARY Higher-level vocabulary and concepts are defined in the glossary.

SandCastle™ would like to hear from you.

Tell us your stories about reading this book. What was your favorite page? Was there something hard that you needed help with? Share the ups and downs of learning to read. To get posted on the ABDO Publishing Company Web site, send us an e-mail at:

sandcastle@abdopublishing.com

Young female cattle are called heifers.
After female cattle have had calves, they
are called cows.

Fiction

Mrs. O'Leary is a proud cow. She is the owner of Moo Town's only ice-cream shop, Cool Licks.

There are many types of cows. The most common dairy cow is the black-and-white Holstein.

Calves and cows from near and far gather here each Saturday for their weekly ice-cream treat. It's a Cattle County tradition.

7

The spots on Holstein cows are unique to each cow. Like snowflakes, no two cows' markings are alike.

No matter how many come,
Mrs. O'Leary knows each of them by
name. "Dottie, I've got a fresh batch of
cherry ice cream just for you! Bessie,
your bowl of chocolate is almost ready."

9

Dairy cows spend up to eight hours a day eating. They drink 25 to 50 gallons of water a day.

Dottie admires Mrs. O'Leary so much that she likes to stay and have a soda after the others have gone. Dottie asks, "Mrs. O'Leary, will you teach me how to make ice cream as wonderful as yours?"

11

Cows do not have top front teeth. Cows grab grass by twisting it around their tongues and pulling it or breaking it with their bottom front teeth.

"Dottie, I'd love to teach you! I'll need the help to get ready for the Moo Town Festival next Saturday," Mrs. O'Leary says. "Come behind the counter and put on an apron. Let's start with those peaches."

13

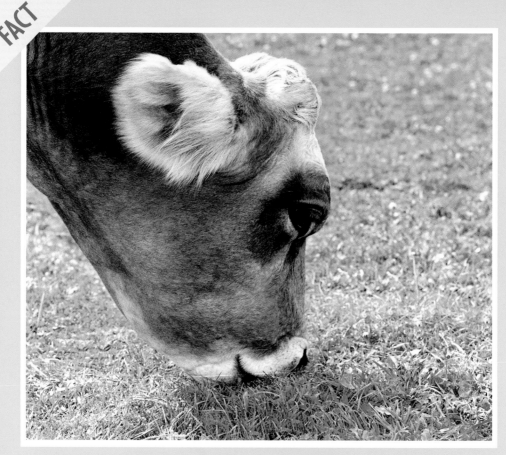

Cows swallow their food whole. It goes into the first of four compartments in their stomachs. Cows regurgitate the resulting cud and chew it.

Dottie washes the peaches and carefully chops them into pieces. She tastes quite a few as she puts them in the bowl. Mrs. O'Leary says, "Dottie, save some for the ice cream!"

A dairy cow that doesn't get enough salt in its diet may lose its appetite and produce less milk. Cows are usually provided with a salt lick.

Mrs. O'Leary adds the sugar, cream, and eggs. Then she packs salt and ice around the container. Dottie cranks the ice-cream maker until she's worn out. "This is hard work!" Dottie exclaims. "Thanks for teaching me how to make ice cream."

17

A tuft of hair that won't lie flat is called a cowlick. Perhaps that's because it looks like hair a cow has licked.

The day of the Moo Town Festival is warm and sunny. Mrs. O'Leary sees Dottie and gives her a big bowl of ice cream.

After she licks the bowl clean, Dottie says, "Wow! This is the best ice cream I've ever had!"

MOO TOWN FESTIVAL

FACT or Fiction?

Read each statement below. Then decide whether it's from the FACT section or the Fiction section!

  1. Cows wear aprons.

  2. Cows spend up to eight hours a day eating.

  3. Cows swallow their food whole.

  4. Cows work at ice-cream stores.

ANSWERS
1. fiction 2. fact 3. fact 4. fiction

Young female cattle are called heifers. After female 8
cattle have had calves, they are called cows. 16

There are many types of cows. The most common 25
dairy cow is the black-and-white Holstein. 33

The spots on Holstein cows are unique to each cow. 43
Like snowflakes, no two cows' markings are alike. 51

Dairy cows spend up to eight hours a day eating. 61
They drink 25 to 50 gallons of water a day. 71

Cows do not have top front teeth. Cows grab grass 81
by twisting it around their tongues and pulling it or 91
breaking it with their bottom front teeth. 98

Cows swallow their food whole. It goes into the first 108
of four compartments in their stomachs. Cows 115
regurgitate the resulting cud and chew it. 122

A dairy cow that doesn't get enough salt in its diet 133
may lose its appetite and produce less milk. Cows are 143
usually provided with a salt lick. 149

A tuft of hair that won't lie flat is called a cowlick. 161
Perhaps that's because it looks like hair a cow has licked. 172

Mrs. O'Leary is a proud cow. She is the owner | 10
of Moo Town's only ice-cream shop, Cool Licks. | 19

Calves and cows from near and far gather | 27
here each Saturday for their weekly ice-cream | 35
treat. It's a Cattle County tradition. | 41

No matter how many come, Mrs. O'Leary | 48
knows each of them by name. "Dottie, I've got a | 58
fresh batch of cherry ice cream just for you! | 67
Bessie, your bowl of chocolate is almost ready." | 75

Dottie admires Mrs. O'Leary so much that she | 83
likes to stay and have a soda after the others | 93
have gone. Dottie asks, "Mrs. O'Leary, will you | 101
teach me how to make ice cream as wonderful as | 111
yours?" | 112

"Dottie, I'd love to teach you! I'll need the help | 122
to get ready for the Moo Town Festival next | 131
Saturday," Mrs. O'Leary says. "Come behind the | 138
counter and put on an apron. Let's start with | 147
those peaches." | 149

Dottie washes the peaches and carefully chops them into pieces. She tastes quite a few as she puts them in the bowl. Mrs. O'Leary says, "Dottie, save some for the ice cream!"

Mrs. O'Leary adds the sugar, cream, and eggs. Then she packs salt and ice around the container. Dottie cranks the ice-cream maker until she's worn out. "This is hard work!" Dottie exclaims. "Thanks for teaching me how to make ice cream."

The day of the Moo Town Festival is warm and sunny. Mrs. O'Leary sees Dottie and gives her a big bowl of ice cream.

After she licks the bowl clean, Dottie says, "Wow! This is the best ice cream I've ever had!"

GLOSSARY

compartment. one of the separate parts of a space that has been divided

cud. food that has been regurgitated

festival. a celebration that happens at the same time each year

regurgitate. to bring food that has already been swallowed back into the mouth

tradition. customs, practices, or beliefs passed from one generation to the next

unique. the only one of its kind

To see a complete list of SandCastle™ books and other nonfiction titles from ABDO Publishing Company, visit www.abdopublishing.com or contact us at: 4940 Viking Drive, Edina, Minnesota 55435 • 1-800-800-1312 • fax: 1-952-831-1632